Wildlife Friends

— NORTHWEST COAST —

GEORGIA A. COCKERHAM

Illustrations by Georgia Cockerham
Book cover photographs by Bruce Cockerham

ISBN: 0989240800
ISBN-13: 9780989240802

Dedication

~~~~~~~~~~~~~~~~~~~~~~~~~~~~

To my wonderful grandchildren whose presence in my life
provides me with both joy and inspiration.

Rozlynn Skye Ward
Kaden Zachary Walker Ward
Natalie Rose Ward

Acknowledgments

〜〜〜〜〜〜〜〜〜〜〜〜〜〜

Thanks to my husband, Bruce, for his patience, gentle
suggestions for the paintings and editing assistance with the poems.

I thank, too, my friend and art instructor Audi Stanton for
both her consistent encouragement that I complete my book,
and her professional critique of my paintings.

THE HARBOR SEAL

The Harbor Seal starts out a pup
His face is cute and round.
With big black eyes and whiskers
He makes a soft "maaaa" sound.

We saw his mama leave him
On the shore to stay awhile
As she swam off to eat enough
For her and hungry child.

Later as the sun went down
The tide came in again and
She came for her pup that
She'd left upon the sand.

Now he lives within the ocean
Where he swims around a lot.
And when he wants to warm up,
Hauls himself upon a rock.

On the rocks the seal pups lie
Above kelp rich and thick.
They seem to live in harmony
Within their coastal clique.

3

CHIPMUNK

The smallest of the squirrel family
And very, very cute,
The Chipmunk scampers about
In his reddish gray striped suit.

He'll run for the peanuts
Grandpa stores in a big tree.
An easy choice of meals,
No work involved—they're free.

He'll stuff his pudgy cheeks
Then to the burrow make a run
To fill his cache with winter food
--No break until he's done.

In the spring he'll find a mate
Or she'll find herself a beau.
Then after 2 to 8 small babes
Each on their own will go.

Colorful stripes and a bushy tail,
Working hard all day.
Stop to drink and find a friend
Then Chipmunk's off to play.

Georgia Cockerham

GEESE

When reading this poem
It's important to note
That it's geese and not a goose
Being written about.

For geese mate for life,
They live as a pair.
And both mom and dad
Of their goslings take care.

Forming a wedge
In formation they fly,
Creating a beautiful
Sight in the sky.

Then a couple break loose
And fly up to the top
Of a nearby sea stack-
Large formation of rock.

Geese are large birds,
Colors gray, white, and black,
Going south in the winter
And in spring flying back.

THE WHALE

On the Oregon coast
It's a whale watching day
When up from the sea
Shoots a 12 foot high spray.

Count 45 seconds
Between each blow and then
With a flip of a tail
To the bottom they'll swim.

Scooping up lots of food
From the ocean's deep floor.
Then back up for some air
Before diving for more.

Each year the Gray Whales
Can be seen as they go,
Migrating from up north
Down to Mexico.

In spring they swim back
To Alaska and then
Next year we'll look forward
To seeing them again.

Georgia Cockerham

9

THE DEER

Carefully walking
One step at a time,
The deer and her fawn
Up the hill they now climb.

Her pretty tan coat
Turns white at the tail
And the fawn with his spots
Still looks a bit frail.

Her coat will darken
As winter draws near,
And his soft antler velvet
Will, in fall, disappear.

Down on the beach
The father buck walks,
Drinking fresh water,
From a stream o'er the rocks.

A family of deer,
Magnificent sight.
Their casual walk
Is for us a delight.

The Hummingbird

Among the smallest of birds
It's a beautiful sight,
Watching a hummingbird
Take off in flight.

Darting right then left,
Straight up and down.
One leaves a tree
Flying round and round.

A break at the feeder
With his long slender bill,
Drinking sugar water
Until reaching his fill.

The sun shines upon
His bright green feathered coat
And a turn of his head
Shows a ruby red throat.

Of all the birds to watch,
I must confess
The Anna Hummingbird
Is one of the best.

Georgia Cockerham

GROUND SQUIRREL

Well "hello" little squirrel,
And how are you today?
You've a beautiful coat
Of white, brown and gray.

I see you've a peanut,
Your favorite snack.
The tree nut house stay's full
To keep you coming back.

Can't eat any more but
More peanuts you take
For the cold winter months
When you'll hibernate.

You dig a small hole
And drop in a nut.
Watching for Blue Jays
While covering it up.

Across the yard
You like to roam.
Then scamper away
Toward your burrow called home.

THE BUTTERFLY

A miracle of nature
Is the butterfly.
Four stages of growth
Allow it to fly.

From egg to larva
A caterpillar is made.
When the pupa is formed,
On a leaf it will stay

Til it opens and
We see what it holds,
A beautiful creature
With wings to unfold.

A symbol for many
Of renewed life,
Nature's gift to us
The Butterfly.

Georgia Cockerham

RIVER OTTER

~~~~~~~~~~~~~~~~~~~

Enjoying the beach on a rock we sit
When our resident Otter swims to shore.
And I think to myself, I must write this down
As my relatives did with their Folk-lore.

He proceeds to walk across the warm sand
In a gait of a crouch before each expand.
I'm reminded of a toy as the wet Otter nears.
He's like a Slinky let go down the stairs.

About every eight steps, he lies on the sand,
Clarifying his needs for both sea and land.
Squirming this way & that as he rolls to & fro,
Drying his fur, putting on quite a show!

Here on the sea, for nothing we lack
With nature our theatre there's always an act.
River Otter by name, to us better known
As one of the reasons we call this our home.

18

www.ingramcontent.com/pod-product-compliance
Lightning Source LLC
Chambersburg PA
CBHW042120040426

42449CB00002B/120